Minute Meditations

by Kay Smith Young

Produced by:

FriesenPress

Suite 300 – 852 Fort Street
Victoria, BC, Canada V8W 1H8

www.friesenpress.com

Distributed to the trade by The Ingram Book Company

All scripture is from the New King James
Version unless otherwise noted.

To my Lord, Jesus Christ,
the Light of my world.

Oh, magnify the Lord with me,

And let us exalt His name together.

(Psalm 34:3)

Thanks to my husband, C.L. Abe Young, who has been my staunchest supporter in all that I have done, and especially in writing this book.

And to Marge McRae, a published friend of mine, who offered valuable information to me.

And to the men's prayer group at New Covenant Fellowship and others who have covered me in prayer throughout this endeavor.

And to my computer-expert friend, Chip Camden, who helped me with that part.

I am most grateful!

INTRODUCTION

Minute Meditations

"Minute" is just a hook. My hope is that you will want to spend more time with the Lord after reading the words printed here; in fact, that these words will be a catalyst to get you going on your own meditation—talking and listening to God. An intimate relationship with God takes time, the same as any other intimate relationship, but a "minute" is better than not having any time with Him. I pray you will be blessed as you consider the scriptures quoted, the praises to the Lord, and the things the Lord impressed upon me. It is all from journals I've kept over the years.

Kay Young

FOREWORD

In the last forty years of pastoral ministry it has been a true joy to work with many men and women of God from whom I have drawn truth and inspiration in my daily walk with them. It is along this line of Christian experience that I find satisfaction in writing the foreword to the book, "Minute Meditations," by the author, Kay Young. I have known Abe and Kay for many, many years and count them as supportive friends in Christ's body of believers.

When Kay asked me to write the foreword to her first book, I was overjoyed to do so. Kay has been a true inspiration to my wife and me and the church we serve. She has a passion for God's word that shows through the devotional quality of her new book. I read the book from cover to cover and enjoyed every page.

In the body of Christ today we are blessed by this kind of work, which helps us grow daily in Christ and challenges us to aspire to intimacy with Him. Don't just rush through the pages of this book, but meditate on them and allow the Holy Spirit to lift you to a higher level in the truth of the Bible. Reflect on how it has impacted Kay and how she wants it to impact us as well. The Bible tells us that "they that wait upon the Lord shall renew their strength," so sit and read and meditate and He will speak to you as He has to Kay..........enjoy.

Pastor Bob Smith
New Covenant Fellowship

<u>John 3:16</u>: For God so loved the world that He gave His only begotten Son, that whoever believes in Him should not perish but have everlasting life.

O, my Father, I thank You for the precious, costly, indescribable, incomprehensible gift of the sacrifice of Your Son for my redemption. A free gift to me that cost <u>You</u> everything! All honor, glory and praise belongs to You, Almighty God, for Your ways, Your love, and Your wisdom. I surrender my life to You, Lord Most High. You alone have place in my heart. Be exalted, O God!

Your thoughts:

_____

_____

_____

_____

_____

_____

_____

_____

<u>Hebrews 12:2a</u>: Looking unto Jesus, the author and finisher of our faith...

Lord Jesus, thank You for Your authority in my life. Thank You for being the author and finisher of my faith. Thank You for Your word, God. I love Your word! You have given me everything I need for life and godliness in Your word. Then You also have given me the Holy Spirit—blessing upon blessing! Holy Spirit, I surrender to Your care, and thank You that You will work in me to conform me to the image of Christ. You are my hope!

Your thoughts:

_____

_____

_____

_____

_____

_____

_____

_____

Psalm 51:10-11: Create in me a clean heart, O God, and renew a steadfast spirit within me. Do not cast me away from Your presence, and do not take Your Holy Spirit from me.

God of wisdom, righteousness, peace, power, deliverance, healing, and mercy, You are the only one who can change my heart and give me a steadfast spirit. I put my trust in You for this work in me. I give You praise and worship because You want to do it! How I love You, Lord; You are my all in all.

Your thoughts:

_____

_____

_____

_____

_____

_____

_____

_____

O, Father, great and mighty are Your works! You did it all and then You take care of it all (Psalm 104). You deliver us out of our troubles and care for us (Psalm 34). What You want back is for us to put off the old and put on the new, walk in the Spirit and be led by the Spirit (Ephesians 4:20). I choose this for me, Father. You are my Lord!

Your thoughts:

_____

_____

_____

_____

_____

_____

_____

_____

<u>Philippians 2:4</u>: Let each of you look out not only for his own interests, but also for the interests of others.

I need to help my husband in what he feels he needs to do, not just be doing my own thing. And, of course, this would include other people as well. Sometimes I am so selfish! Thank You for sending me to this verse, Lord.

Your thoughts:

_____

_____

_____

_____

_____

_____

_____

_____

Psalm 52:8-9: But I am like a green olive tree in the house of God; I trust in the mercy of God forever and ever. I will praise You forever, because You have done it. And in the presence of Your saints I will wait on Your name, for it is good.

You have done it all: drawn me to Jesus, called, chosen, saved me, and are always teaching, leading, correcting me. I do praise you, Father. And I will wait on Your name, for it is good.

Your thoughts:

_____

_____

_____

_____

_____

_____

_____

_____

James 1:23-24: Anyone who listens to the word but does not do what it says is like a man who looks at his face in a mirror and, after looking at himself, goes away and immediately forgets what he looks like.

Lord, I'm halfway through the book of James. I was reminded of this verse this morning in my devotions and it made me think about what I'm doing with what I've gone over. I do my lesson each day, but how am I letting it impact and change me? Holy Spirit, help me be a doer of the Word and not a hearer only. How I need You, Jesus!

Your thoughts:

_____

_____

_____

_____

_____

_____

_____

_____

Psalm 85:10,13: Mercy and truth have met together, righteous-ness and peace have kissed. Righteousness will go before Him, and shall make His footsteps our pathway.

Mercy and truth have met together in Jesus—the same for righ-teousness and peace. I want His footsteps to be my path. There I am safe and have nothing to fear. I look to the Lord, who is my provider and my protector—

Jesus, the One and Only;

Jesus, the Righteous One;

Jesus, the Prince of Peace.

Your thoughts:

_____

_____

_____

_____

_____

_____

_____

_____

Matthew 11:28-30: Come to Me, all You who labor and are heavy laden, and I will give you rest. Take My yoke upon you and learn of Me, for I am gentle and lowly in heart, and you will find rest for your souls. For My yoke is easy and My burden is light.

Thank You, Lord, for Your promise of rest when we come to You, regardless of where we are or what we're going through. You are our refuge, our peace, our strength. You want us to commit all to you and be at rest. Thank You that Your yoke is easy and Your burden is light.

Your thoughts:

_____

_____

_____

_____

_____

_____

_____

_____

Esther 5:2: So it was, when the king saw Queen Esther stand-ing in the court, that she found favor in his sight, and the king held out to Esther the golden scepter that was in his hand. Then Esther went near and touched the top of the scepter.

King Jesus, help me to remember that You are holding out the golden scepter to me and I but need to reach out and touch it to be in Your presence and spend time with You. Help me to do it! Thank You for wanting to spend time with me. What an awesome thing!

Your thoughts:

_____

_____

_____

_____

_____

_____

_____

Ephesians 4:4-6: There is one body and one Spirit, just as you were called in one hope of your calling; one Lord, one faith, one baptism; one God and Father of all, who is above all, and through all, and in you all.

I stop my busy thoughts and plans, Lord; I acknowledge You, God, my Father; Jesus, my Savior and Lord; Holy Spirit, my comforter, teacher, and guide. You are holy, Lord, and I worship You as the One and Only, My All-in-All, the Lord Most High, Almighty God.

Your thoughts:

_____

_____

_____

_____

_____

_____

_____

_____

Psalm 32:8: I will instruct you and teach you in the way you should go; I will guide you with My eye.

Psalm 48:14: For this is God, our God forever and ever; He will be our guide even to death.

Thank You, God, for Your promises to instruct, teach, and guide us. Whatever You have for me, Father, my trust is in You. Praise Your name for Your care and faithfulness—always, in all things! Your faithfulness increases my faith.

Your thoughts:

_____

_____

_____

_____

_____

_____

_____

_____

In the New Testament, the first two things Jesus said were:

"Repent, for the kingdom of heaven is at hand." Matthew 4:17

"Follow Me, and I will make you fishers of men." Matthew 4:19

I need to pay more attention to what Jesus says. I want to continue in submission, teachability, and shapeability. I thank the Lord that He will do through me what He wants done, if I remain submitted to Him. I don't have to fret as long as my focus is on Jesus—what a blessing!

Your thoughts:

_____

_____

_____

_____

_____

_____

_____

<u>Philippians 4:8</u>: Finally brethren,

whatever things are true,

whatever things are noble,

whatever things are just,

whatever things are pure,

whatever things are lovely,

whatever things are of good report,

if there is any virtue and if there is anything praiseworthy—meditate on these things.

So, don't let the negatives of fear, anxiety, torment, dread, and un-ease have any part in my thinking. Get rid of them as soon as they pop up and turn to praise; meditate on the above good things. No place given to the enemy!

Your thoughts:

_____

_____

_____

_____

_____

_____

_____

_____

<u>Psalm 43:5</u>: Why are you cast down, O my soul? And why are you disquieted within me? Hope in God, for I shall yet praise Him, the help of my countenance and my God.

Things are not always rosy. We have ups and downs like everyone does. But God is always there to help us when we reach out to Him. The trick is to do it right away instead of being miserable for a long time first. He's faithful! Praise His name!

Your thoughts:

_____

_____

_____

_____

_____

_____

_____

_____

Romans 6:13: And do not present your members as instruments of unrighteousness to sin, but present yourselves to God as being alive from the dead, and your members as instruments of righteousness to God.

God, I present my mind (what I think), my eyes (what I look at), my ears (what I listen to), my heart (the issues of my life), my hands (what I touch), and my feet (where I go), to You as instruments of righteousness. I present my body a living sacrifice to You as my reasonable service of worship. (Romans 12:1)

Your thoughts:

_____

_____

_____

_____

_____

_____

_____

_____

Lamentations 3:24: "The Lord is my portion," says my soul. "Therefore I hope in Him!"

God gives me hope. I can always have hope because He gives it to me. I need to look for it. Be aware of it. Be happy for it. Each new day can bring me new hope if I look for and expect it. I can rest in that and be at peace. God has my back!

Your thoughts:

_____

_____

_____

_____

_____

_____

_____

I cried out to God that we need Jesus to come—we are not of this world and we are not doing well <u>in</u> it. But…God is with us; it is enough! He gave me:

<u>Psalm 46:1-2</u>: God is our refuge and strength, a very present help in trouble. Therefore we will not fear, even though the Earth be removed and though the mountains be carried into the midst of the sea; though its waters roar and be troubled, though the mountains shake with its swelling. <u>Verse 7</u>: The Lord of hosts is with us; the God of Jacob is our refuge. <u>Verse 10a</u>: Be still and know that I am God.

Your thoughts:

_____

_____

_____

_____

_____

_____

_____

_____

<u>Ephesians 1:4</u>: ...just as He [God] chose us in Him [Christ] before the foundation of the world, that we should be holy and without blame before Him in love...

That the God of the universe would choose me to be part of His family is overwhelming to me. I weep whenever I really think about it. It has changed my life completely to be so valued by God. I never knew I had value until meeting the Lord Jesus Christ. Jesus has healed me—spirit, soul, body! How I thank You, Lord!

Your thoughts:

_____

_____

_____

_____

_____

_____

_____

_____

Psalm 145:9: The Lord is good to all, and His tender mercies are over all His works.

Thank You for Your mercies that are new every morning, Lord. How we need Your mercy, God. You are a good, faithful, loving, wise Father, and I praise and honor You. Amen!

Your thoughts:

_____

_____

_____

_____

_____

_____

_____

_____

<u>2 Corinthians 1:3-4</u>: Blessed be the God and Father of our Lord Jesus Christ, the Father of mercies and God of all comfort, who comforts us in all our tribulation, that we may be able to comfort those who are in any trouble, with the comfort which we ourselves are comforted by God.

O God, how many times you have comforted me through those who have been through the fire! And, God, You have also used me to comfort others with the same comfort You saw that I received. Your ways are so good, Lord—they make me want to surrender everything to You!

Your thoughts:

_____

_____

_____

_____

_____

_____

_____

_____

Psalm 119:105: Your Word is a lamp to my feet and a light to my path.

I'm so grateful for Your Word and the power in it, Lord. Truly it is a lamp for my path. You teach me, correct me, challenge me, admonish me, and encourage me through it every day. There is something new to learn every time I read it. I am greatly blessed in so many ways by Your Word, Father, I can scarcely take it in!

Your thoughts:

_____

_____

_____

_____

_____

_____

_____

_____

<u>1 Corinthians 1:9</u>: God is faithful, by whom you were called into the fellowship of His Son, Jesus Christ our Lord.

Lord God, I acknowledge that You have called me, and that it is because of You that I am in Christ. I am so grateful, Father, that You saw fit to call me. It makes me want to please You, God, and I pray for holiness in my life.

Your thoughts:

_____

_____

_____

_____

_____

_____

_____

_____

Psalm 54:4, 6a (NIV): Surely God is my help; the Lord is the one who sustains me. I will praise Your name, O Lord, for it is good.

*God, You are my God, and I will ever
praise You! You are gracious,*

forgiving,

merciful,

and kind.

*I love and appreciate Your goodness to me, Lord.
I am so blessed that You are my Father.*

Your thoughts:

_____

_____

_____

_____

_____

_____

_____

_____

Revelation 1:8: "I am the Alpha and the Omega, the Beginning and the End," says the Lord, "who is and who was and who is to come, the Almighty."

Lord, I thank You that You are the Alpha and Omega, the Beginning and the End. To him who is thirsty, You will give to drink without cost from the spring of the water of life. I am thirsty, Lord, and I come to You to know You more.

Your thoughts:

_____

_____

_____

_____

_____

_____

_____

God spoke in my spirit, "O, precious child of Mine, be at rest, be at peace, for you have a Father who watches over you. No worries, no fears, for I AM! Not 'I am thus and so' but just I AM (Exodus 3:14). And that is all you need."

Thank You, Lord, for Your loving kindness and Your mercies that are new every morning. You are a God of peace, a God of justice. I give You honor and praise!

Your thoughts:

_____

_____

_____

_____

_____

_____

_____

_____

Matthew 16:24: Then Jesus said to His disciples, "If anyone desires to come after Me, let him deny himself, and take up his cross, and follow Me."

I repent of self-concern, Lord, and ask Your forgiveness. It is my desire to go deeper with You. I pray You will show me what You want to do through me by the Holy Spirit, that I will hear You clearly, and that Holy Spirit will help me to be obedient. Jesus, I want You to be Lord of every area of my life.

Your thoughts:

_____

_____

_____

_____

_____

_____

_____

_____

I asked, "What is on <u>Your</u> heart today, Lord?"

I felt that He replied, "My people. My people are always on My heart. I have so much more for ALL of you, but you seem to not want it, or expect it, or you're afraid. There is no reason to fear—all good gifts come from Me. Bad things come from the enemy of your soul. Stand against him as I have instructed you in My Word. It is safe to trust Me as I have your good on My heart and in My plans. I will correct you and I will change you, but I won't harm you. Come to Me. Abide in Me. I will begin to show you what more I have for you."

Your thoughts:

_____
_____
_____
_____
_____
_____
_____
_____
_____
_____
_____
_____
_____

The Lord sent me to <u>Psalm 104,</u> *and after I had read it, He impressed upon me:*

"In this Psalm I wanted you to see that I AM powerful and I AM in control. Because of that you need have no fear, but rest in Me, for I will take care of you. My ways are pure. I AM conforming you into the image of My Son. Don't be discouraged; it is a process. Rest in Me. Trust Me."

Your thoughts:

_____

_____

_____

_____

_____

_____

_____

_____

Romans 8:15: For you did not receive the spirit of bondage again to fear, but you received the Spirit of adoption by whom we cry out, "Abba, Father."

Father, I remember the day when I surrendered everything to You and asked You to take over my life. The little word "Abba" began running around inside my head, but I didn't know what it meant. It wasn't until I got to Romans 8:15 in reading through the Bible after that day that I saw "Abba" written out and what it meant. My gratitude to You for adopting me into Your family is bigger than I know how to express. I give You, once again, my life in response to just thinking about it.

Your thoughts:

_____

_____

_____

_____

_____

_____

_____

<u>Psalm 124:8</u>: My help is in the name of the Lord, the Maker of Heaven and Earth.

Father God, I'm so grateful that You want to help us, that You want us to call upon You for help. I say, "Help, Lord!" a lot and I'm glad to know it's okay. It is amazing that the Lord, the Maker of Heaven and Earth, wants to help me—but here it is. I thank You, Lord, for Your love and mercy extended to us.

Your thoughts:

_____

_____

_____

_____

_____

_____

_____

_____

From Revelation 1, several things stand out about God and His ways:

God, Who is, and Who was, and Who is to come; Jesus, firstborn from the dead and the ruler of the kings of the Earth.

He has freed us from our sins by His blood, and has made us to be a kingdom and priests to serve His God and Father. He is the Alpha and the Omega, Who is, Who was, and Who is to come; the Almighty. He is the First and the Last and the Living One. He was dead, and behold! He is alive for ever and ever. He holds the keys of death and Hades.

Your thoughts:

_____

_____

_____

_____

_____

_____

_____

_____

Psalm 36:5-6 (NIV): Your love, O Lord, reaches to the heavens, Your faithfulness to the skies. Your righteousness is like the mighty mountains, Your justice like the great deep.

Lord Jesus, You are

The Bread of life,

The Door,

The Gate,

Very God of very God,

The Vine,

The great Shepherd.

Your ways are love, joy, peace, and justice. I can rest in You for You have my good in mind.

Your thoughts:

_____

_____

_____

_____

_____

_____

_____

<u>Proverbs 3:5-6</u>: Trust in the Lord with all your heart, and lean not on your own understanding; in all your ways acknowledge Him, and He shall direct your paths.

God, I can trust in You with all my heart and lean not on my own understanding because You are love; Your ways are love. You are peace; Your ways are peace. You are my Lord, Savior, Master, Brother, Lover of my soul, Friend, and the Strong Tower I can run into.

Your thoughts:

_____

_____

_____

_____

_____

_____

_____

From the Lord for today: "Sunshine, clouds, rain—it really doesn't matter. I am on the throne and ALL is well. Your trust is in Me and I respond to that and you are blessed. No worries, no fears, just perfect peace because I AM a God of peace. You belong to Me. I am yours and you are Mine, my child, the love of My heart. Rest in Me. I will direct your path. I will heal your body. Do not fret! Keep going! I have more for you. Don't let discouragement rob you of joy. I AM your joy. Let it ALL just be and keep trusting. Father will take care of you, My child. You are truly blessed because you belong to Me. Relax. Let go. I will direct. Then respond."

Your thoughts:

_____

_____

_____

_____

_____

_____

_____

Jesus, today in Luke I read about Your conception (a miracle!), Your birth,

Simeon and Anna recognizing You when Your parents took You to the temple,

You sitting with the teachers in the temple and asking them questions at age twelve,

Your genealogy,

Your temptations in the wilderness,

and the beginning of Your ministry, including healing, casting out demons, and preaching the good news.

WOW!

Your thoughts:

_____

_____

_____

_____

_____

_____

_____

_____

<u>Psalm 104</u>: *How God created everything and how He sustains everything. All praise and honor to God Almighty!*

From the Lord: "You are beautiful in My sight because you are My creation. I will take care of you just as you read in Psalm 104—all things are under My care. I AM the faithful One—put your trust in Me for all things. Release every concern to Me that I may work on it. Trust Me in all things. Trust Me. I care for you!"

Your thoughts:

_____

_____

_____

_____

_____

_____

_____

_____

1John 3:1a: Behold what manner of love the Father has bestowed on us, that we should be called children of God!

God, I thank You for the privilege of calling You Father. I thank You for the nurturing, encouragement, discipline, forgiveness, and love that You give me. You have changed my life completely since I turned it completely over to You. I am blessed beyond measure and very grateful. I pray my life would truly be to the praise of Your glory for You work all things for my good. I trust You implicitly!

Your thoughts:

_____

_____

_____

_____

_____

_____

_____

_____

Psalm 102:12 (NIV): "But You, O Lord, sit enthroned forever; Your renown endures through all generations."

Lord, You are the Word; You are Truth; You are sovereign. It doesn't even matter if people believe this or not; it is true. You are so far above us, Lord, it is a miracle that You pay any attention to us at all—but thank You that You do. All glory to You, Lord—glory in the highest!

Your thoughts:

_____

_____

_____

_____

_____

_____

_____

_____

James 1:2-3: "My brethren, count it all joy when you fall into various trials, knowing that the testing of your faith produces patience." The New Daily Study Bible (Wm. Barclay) says about this, "The aim of testing is to purge us of all impurity." And, "By the way in which we meet every experience in life, we are making ourselves either fit or unfit for the task which God meant us to do."

"I" (meaning myself) can't do it. "I" fail all the time. The only hope I have is that Jesus will give me His purity, His love, His faith, Himself. And that He will live out His life in me.

Your thoughts:

_____

_____

_____

_____

_____

_____

_____

_____

Genesis 4:7: ...And if you do not do well, sin lies at the door. And its desire is for [toward] you, BUT YOU SHOULD RULE OVER IT!

This is what God said to Cain, but surely it is the same for all of us. Am I ruling over sin? Am I even conscious of sin in my life? Search my heart, O God; convict me, Holy Spirit.

Your thoughts:

_____

_____

_____

_____

_____

_____

_____

Revelation 3:15: "I know your works, that you are neither cold nor hot. I could wish you were cold or hot."

Today I prayed God would crush indifference in me, my family, my church, and community. Apathy has a stranglehold on us that we need to break. To God be the glory, He is able!

Your thoughts:

_____

_____

_____

_____

_____

_____

_____

_____

Psalm 85:8: I will hear what the Lord will speak, for He will speak peace to His people and to His saints; but let them not turn back to folly.

I stop my busy thoughts and plans, Lord, and quit thinking about what is coming tomorrow. I acknowledge You, God—my Father, Jesus—my Savior and Lord, and Holy Spirit—my Comforter, Teacher, and Guide. Resting in You is the only way to peace. All else truly is folly!

Your thoughts:

_____

_____

_____

_____

_____

_____

_____

_____

<u>Ephesians 2:12-13 (NIV)</u>: ...

remember that at that time you were separate from Christ... without hope and without God in the world. But now in Christ Jesus you who once were far away have been brought near through the blood of Christ.

God, I can vividly remember the days, months, and years before I asked You to take over my life completely. Those were miserable, wretched, and depressed days; truly without hope. Thank You from my heart that You made me part of Your family. Thank You that You continue to show me through the Word who You are, that I might really know You. You're my Father, who brought me near to Yourself!

Your thoughts:

_____

_____

_____

_____

_____

_____

_____

_____

_____

<u>Psalm 28:1</u>: Blessed is everyone who fears the Lord, who walks in His ways.

Whatever you have for me, Father, my trust is in You. I praise Your Name for Your care and faithfulness, always, in all things. I don't have to know or do, I just need to be. I come to You, Jesus, as You asked us to: "Come unto Me and I will give you rest."

Your thoughts:

_____

_____

_____

_____

_____

_____

_____

_____

Isaiah 33:6a (NET): He is your constant source of stability.

O, God, how I need this—how I need You! Everywhere I turn, so much I hear and read is just the opposite: instability. We don't know what is happening in America or in the world; both seem to have turned their backs on You. But God, You are our peace, wisdom, help, provision, and hope. We can rely on You because You are faithful. You love us and care for us. How I thank You that I belong to You, my Abba Father.

Your thoughts:

_____

_____

_____

_____

_____

_____

_____

_____

<u>Psalm 41:1 (NIV)</u>: Blessed is he who has regard for the weak; the Lord delivers Him in times of trouble.

The weak could be the young, the old, the more frail, those in emotional upheaval, the sick, the poor, the homeless, or those in the womb—the most dangerous place to be today. God, I pray You would give me a heart that regards the weak and that You would give me wisdom to know what is my part.

Your thoughts:

_____

_____

_____

_____

_____

_____

_____

_____

<u>Proverbs 18:10</u>: The name of the Lord is a strong tower; the righteous run to it and are safe.

Jehovah-jireh: the Lord will provide

Jehovah-rapha: the Lord has healed

Jehovah-nissi: the Lord my banner

Jehovah-shalom: the Lord is peace

Jehovah-tsidkenu: the Lord our righteousness

Jehovah-rohi: the Lord our shepherd

Jehovah-shamma: the Lord is there

What more could we possibly want or need?

Your thoughts:

_____

_____

_____

_____

_____

_____

_____

_____

<u>Psalm 19:14</u>: Let the words of my mouth and the meditation of my heart be acceptable in Your sight, O Lord, my strength and my Redeemer.

*That is my prayer, Lord. I bring to You, and lay at Your feet, all the disquieting and critical thoughts that run through my head at times. I pray that You would change me and them. You want us to think on the true, noble, just, pure, lovely, of good report, virtuous, and praiseworthy (*Philippians 4:8*). God, I fully surrender to You. Jesus, I pray You would live out Your very life in me.*

Your thoughts:

_____

_____

_____

_____

_____

_____

_____

_____

<u>Psalm 43:3</u>: Oh, send out Your light and Your truth! Let them lead me; let them bring me to Your holy hill and to Your tabernacle.

What great need we have for Your light and truth, Father God. Your word is a light to our path (Ps. 119:105) and all of Your word is truth (Ps. 119:160). I picture myself walking around in this bubble of light wherever I'm going (in Jesus, the Light of the world), and as long as I go to the word for it, I have truth as the answer to my questions. Thank You!

Your thoughts:

_____

_____

_____

_____

_____

_____

_____

_____

<u>Hebrews 12:11 (NIV)</u>: No discipline seems pleasant at the time, but painful. Later on, however, it produces a harvest of righteousness and peace for those who have been trained by it.

God, I pray for Your discipline and training in my life. Correct me, change me, convict me, conform me to the image of Christ. I pray I would do nothing to hinder Your work in me! I am so grateful every day for my life and what You are doing in it.

Your thoughts:

_____

_____

_____

_____

_____

_____

_____

_____

<u>Psalm 68:4</u>: Sing to God, sing praises to His name; extol Him who rides on the clouds, by His name Yah, and rejoice before Him.

Holy, worthy Lord, I do praise Your name. All honor belongs to You, God. There is no one like our God! Thank You for Your loving kindness, mercy, grace, forgiveness, wisdom, plans, and purposes for Your people. My trust is in You, Lord, because You are faithful, and You do all things well. I rejoice before You. Jesus, I shout Your name over everything to do with my life! You are LORD over me and all that has to do with me.

Your thoughts:

_____

_____

_____

_____

_____

_____

_____

_____

1 John 4:18: There is no fear in love, but perfect love casts out fear, because fear involves torment. But he who fears has not been made perfect in love.

It is not our perfect love that casts out fear, but Your perfect love. Holy God, Lord Jesus, blessed Holy Spirit: Your ways are perfect, Your wisdom unsearchable. You are powerful, holy, just, and loving—worthy of all praise, honor, glory, and blessing. I bow before You, God. "Thank You" seems little to say, but You alone have done it all!

Your thoughts:

_____

_____

_____

_____

_____

_____

_____

Psalm 63:3: Because Your loving kindness is better than life, my lips shall praise You.

I do praise You, Abba Father, great and mighty God. You alone are worthy of praise and worship. Someday all the Earth will acknowledge You in worship because they will recognize who You are. May that time come quickly, Lord Jesus!

Your thoughts:

_____

_____

_____

_____

_____

_____

_____

_____

<u>Jude 1:24-25</u>: Now to Him who is able to keep you from stumbling, and to present you faultless before the presence of His glory with exceeding joy, to God our Savior, who alone is wise, be glory and majesty, dominion and power, both now and forever. Amen.

O, God, my Father, the more I know You, the more I'm aware of failures in my life. How wonderful to know that You are able and willing to keep me from stumbling. May the Holy Spirit remind me of this before I make a wrong choice, take a wrong turn, say a mean word, be unloving to anyone, or criticize. I love You, Lord Jesus, and I exalt Your holy name. Thank You that presenting me faultless in the Father's presence brings <u>You</u> joy

Your thoughts:

_____

_____

_____

_____

_____

_____

_____

_____

Psalm 1:1-2: Blessed is the man who walks not in the counsel of the ungodly, nor stands in the path of sinners, nor sits in the seat of the scornful; but his delight is in the law of the Lord, and in His law he meditates day and night.

Yesterday I started a book by an author I usually like, but it had stuff in it I didn't want to read, for it would be walking in the counsel of the ungodly. The book went into the trash and I thank You, God, for Your Word, which instructs us in the way we should go. Thank You, Holy Spirit, for Your checks and balances.

Your thoughts:

_____

_____

_____

_____

_____

_____

_____

_____

<u>James 1:5</u>: If any of you lacks wisdom, let him ask of God, who gives to all liberally and without reproach, and it will be given to him.

Lord, I ask You for wisdom—Your wisdom that leads us to be pure, friendly, gentle, sensible, kind, helpful, genuine, and sincere. Please give me Your grace to live right and be humble and wise in everything I do. Your Word says fear of the Lord is the beginning of wisdom and I choose the fear of the Lord with respect, reverence, and awe of You.

Your thoughts:

_____

_____

_____

_____

_____

_____

_____

_____

<u>Psalm 57:5</u>: Be exalted, O God, above the heavens; let Your glory be above all the Earth.

You alone, God, are worthy of all glory, praise, and honor! Your ways are just, perfect, wise, and loving. Thank You, Lord, for drawing me unto Jesus, forgiving my sins, saving me, and bringing me into Your family, kingdom, church, and body. Thank You for Your plans and purposes for me.

I give You full sway in my life and pray You will be the BOSS!

Your thoughts:

_____

_____

_____

_____

_____

_____

_____

_____

<u>Job 2:3</u>: Then the Lord said to Satan, "Have you considered My servant Job, that there is none like him on the Earth, a blameless and upright man, one who fears God and shuns evil? And still he holds fast to his integrity, although you incited Me against him, to destroy him without cause."

Father God, I pray for integrity in all areas of my life, that You would grow me into being blameless and upright, fearing You and turning away from evil. I pray for integrity when things are not so good as well as when things are wonderful. May Your grace abound toward me for integrity in my heart—no compromises in my life. Amen!

Your thoughts:

_____

_____

_____

_____

_____

_____

_____

Psalm 24:3-4: Who may ascend into the hill of the Lord? Or who may stand in His holy place? He who has clean hands and a pure heart. Who has not lifted up his soul to an idol, nor sworn deceitfully.

Lord, I pray for clean hands and a pure heart, and that I do not lift up my soul to an idol, nor swear deceitfully. An idol is probably anything that takes more of my time than You, Lord. And if I say to You that I'm not going to do or say certain things any more, but then I do, I have sworn deceitfully. How I need You, Jesus and Holy Spirit. Help, Lord! Die, flesh! Live through me, Jesus.

Your thoughts:

_____

_____

_____

_____

_____

_____

_____

_____

Philippians 1:6: ...being confident of this very thing, that He who has begun a good work in you will complete it until the day of Jesus Christ.

Philippians 2:13: ...for it is God who works in you both to will and to do for His good pleasure.

God, I'm so grateful for these two scriptures. Sometimes I get discouraged because I'm still making mistakes and wrong choices when I should be past that at my age. The truth is we'll never be perfect until Jesus comes back, and I must rely on Him to keep moving me forward in the realm of the Spirit.

Your thoughts:

_____

_____

_____

_____

_____

_____

_____

<u>Psalm 54:1a</u>: Save me, O God, by Your name...

Your name, God, represents Your covenant-keeping character. Your name is a strong tower I can run into and be safe (Proverbs 18:10). I'm to fear this glorious and awesome name, THE LORD YOUR GOD (Deuteronomy 28:58). Our Redeemer from Everlasting is His name (Isaiah 63:16). Your name is above every name (Philippians 2:9). Praise Your name, Mighty God!

Your thoughts:

_____

_____

_____

_____

_____

_____

_____

_____

<u>Jeremiah 29:11</u>: For I know the thoughts that I think toward you, says the Lord, thoughts of peace and not of evil, to give you a future and a hope.

What a blessing to know that You have thoughts toward me, Lord. How I need Your peace! My life and times are in Your hands, God. You are my future and my hope. My life became new when I met Jesus as Savior. How I thank You for saving me, Lord! You are a good God!

Your thoughts:

_____

_____

_____

_____

_____

_____

_____

_____

<u>Psalm 52:1b</u>: The goodness of God endures continually.

<u>Psalm 52:8-9</u>: But I am like a green olive tree in the house of God; I trust in the mercy of God forever and ever. I will praise You forever because You have done it, and in the presence of Your saints I will wait on Your name, for it is good.

I pray to be more willing to speak out about our great God, who He is and what He has done for us—be BOLD about it! People need to know. I pray to be more devoted to Him; to remember each morning to Whom I belong; let being a Christian define who I am, how I think, what I feel; lead a godly life in this world.

Your thoughts:

_____

_____

_____

_____

_____

_____

_____

_____

*LORD, I ask You and trust You for the quali-
ties You desire in me from* <u>2 Peter 1:5-7</u>*:*

faith,

virtue,

knowledge,

self-control,

perseverance,

godliness,

brotherly kindness,

and love.

*I cannot produce these in myself but I can, and do, sur-
render to You to do it in me. And I can read Your word
and pray, whereby You show me what is needed.*

Your thoughts:

_____

_____

_____

_____

_____

_____

_____

_____

<u>Psalm 139:23-24</u>: Search me, O God, and know my heart; try me and know my anxieties; And see if there is any wicked way in me, and lead me in the way everlasting.

Reveal to me what is in my heart that needs to be dealt with, Lord. I want to wake up to You, God, and experience You. I bend my knee to You, Lord. Holy Spirit, I pray You would touch my heart and set it afire for God.

Your thoughts:

_____

_____

_____

_____

_____

_____

_____

_____

Isaiah 58:6-7: Is this not the fast that I have chosen: to loose the bonds of wickedness, to undo the heavy burdens, to let the oppressed go free, and that you break every yoke? Is it not to share your bread with the hungry, and that you bring to your house the poor who are cast out; when you see the naked, that you cover him, and not hide yourself from your own flesh?

God, You told me this would be my lifetime verse. I pray for Your compassion to be in me, to work through me. I give you my body, a living sacrifice; my eyes for Your tears; my mouth for Your prayers; my hands for Your touch; my feet for Your journeys; my emotions for Your feelings; my mind for Your thoughts; and my will for Your will to be done on Earth as it is in Heaven.

Your thoughts:

_____

_____

_____

_____

_____

_____

_____

_____

Ephesians 4:29,31: Let no corrupt word proceed out of your mouth, but what is good for necessary edification, that it may impart grace to the hearers. Let all bitterness, wrath, anger, clamor (loud quarreling), and evil speaking be put away from you, with all malice.

WOW, Father, You certainly sent me to the right chapter! I need You to conquer my tongue, Lord, for I do (say) what I don't want to, and don't do (say) what I do want to. I submit my tongue to You, Lord, and pray for Your check before I open my mouth to say any harmful thing. Thank You for being such a personal God, who knows us so well and corrects when we are not pleasing You. It's what a loving Father does!

Your thoughts:

_____

_____

_____

_____

_____

_____

_____

_____

<u>Psalm 49:15</u>: ...God will redeem my soul from the power of the grave, for He shall receive me. Selah.

Lord, our lives and times are in Your hands—the only safe place to be! And to be absent from these bodies is to be present with You, so we can't lose either way. You are such a precious, personal God I can scarcely grab onto it. You are <u>amazing,</u> really. I love You, Lord.

Your thoughts:

_____

_____

_____

_____

_____

_____

_____

_____

<u>John 20:21</u>: [Jesus said,] "As the Father has sent Me, so send I you."

I was vacuuming one long-ago day and suddenly felt I had to get on my knees and pray. The prayer that came out of my mouth was, "If there is one verse You want me to understand, what is it?" The answer was, "John 20:21." I've thought about it a lot and the conclusion I came to was that Luke 4:18b-19 was the way the Father sent Jesus: "He has sent Me to heal the brokenhearted, to proclaim liberty to the captives and recovery of sight to the blind, to set at liberty those who are oppressed; to proclaim the acceptable year of the Lord." I believe this is what God wants of us as well.

Your thoughts:

_____

_____

_____

_____

_____

_____

_____

_____

_____

Psalm 42:2 (NIV): My soul thirsts for God, the living God. When can I go and meet with God?

I thank You, Lord, that I can meet with You anytime, <u>anywhere</u>. By Your precious Spirit You are always with me and we can talk to each other whenever I take the time. So I can't complain, Lord; if we're not communicating, it's my fault, not Yours!

Your thoughts:

_____

_____

_____

_____

_____

_____

_____

_____

<u>Exodus 20:2</u>: "I am the Lord your God, who brought you out of the land of Egypt, out of the house of bondage."

Do I believe and know You as the One and Only God? Have I allowed You to bring me out of the slavery, the bondages of my life? Am I willing to allow You to deal with anything and everything that keeps me from the very best You have for me, that keeps me from Your freedom in any way? Lord, I pray You would make sure the answer to all these questions is a resounding "YES."

Your thoughts:

_____

_____

_____

_____

_____

_____

_____

_____

Psalm 42:5 (NIV): Why are you downcast, O my soul? Why so disturbed within me? Put your hope in God, for I will yet praise Him, my Savior and my God.

The problem and the answer wrapped up in one verse—what a blessing! God, Your ways are perfect. Thank You for Your word, which contains the answer for every problem we encounter.

Your thoughts:

_____

_____

_____

_____

_____

_____

_____

_____

<u>James 4:14a, 15 (NIV)</u>: Why, you do not even know what will happen tomorrow. Instead, you ought to say, "If it is the Lord's will, we will live and do this or that."

This reminds me of something we learned in summer family camp years ago: pray that you live every day God planned for you to live and that He prepares your soul and spirit to be with Him throughout eternity. All praise, honor, and glory to You, Sovereign Lord. You alone are God! My life and times are in Your hands and there are safe.

Your thoughts:

_____

_____

_____

_____

_____

_____

_____

<u>Acts 4:29-30 (paraphrased)</u>: Now, Lord...grant to Your servant, Kay, that with all boldness I may speak Your word, by stretching out Your hand to heal, and that signs and wonders may be done through the name of Your holy Servant Jesus.

This was my prayer when I went to Sierra Leone and then the next year to Malawi and it was to and for Your glory, Lord, and that others would believe. You did marvelous things in New Testament days to interest people in what Jesus had to say. I believe it should be the same today. Not to pump people up, but to show that You cared enough to heal, deliver, and save—and You are still doing that!

Your thoughts:

_____

_____

_____

_____

_____

_____

_____

_____

Psalm 47:1-2 (NIV): Clap your hands, all you nations; shout to God with cries of joy. How awesome is the Lord Most High, the great King over all the Earth!

God, You are still King over all the Earth! Your reign is forever. Someday all people will recognize Your Lordship. I'm so grateful that You are my Lord now and I can know You now. I sing praises to Your name for You are great and greatly to be praised. Hallelujah!

Your thoughts:

_____

_____

_____

_____

_____

_____

_____

_____

<u>Acts 1:4-5</u>: And being assembled together with them, He commanded them not to depart from Jerusalem, but to wait for the Promise of the Father, "Which," He said, "you have heard from Me; for John truly baptized with water, but you shall be baptized with the Holy Spirit not many days from now."

Jesus, I pray You would fill me to overflowing with the Spirit of the Lord. Any real ministry will come from this overflow. The baptism in the power of the Holy Spirit is what enables us to lead lives pleasing to You, Lord, and to witness to those who don't yet know You. I think we have set this aside far too much for this day and age. We need it now more than ever. Lord, please take charge in this and accomplish <u>Your</u> plans and purposes. May we fall in with them!

Your thoughts:

_____

_____

_____

_____

_____

_____

_____

_____

<u>Psalm 18:1-2</u>: I will love You, O Lord, my strength. The Lord is my rock and my fortress and my deliverer; my God, my strength, in whom I will trust; my shield and the horn of my salvation, my stronghold.

God, You are all these things to me and I count on You for each of them in my life. I praise You, for Your ways are perfect. Thank You for being my Abba Father and caring for me as Your child. You are everything to me.

Your thoughts:

_____

_____

_____

_____

_____

_____

_____

_____

Romans 12:2: And do not be conformed to the world, but be transformed by the renewing of your mind, that you may prove what is that good and acceptable and perfect will of God.

These are instructions from Paul to me. I need to make a choice first of all, and then ask God to help me do it. "Not be conformed to the world" is so far-reaching I can't fathom all of it at this point. I can only begin with what I know and expect that God will keep showing me as we move along. This will be a life-time work. The more my mind is renewed through the Word and prayer and by the Holy Spirit, the more I'll be transformed and the less I'll be conformed to the world. Let it be, dear Lord. Amen and amen!

Your thoughts:

_____

_____

_____

_____

_____

_____

_____

_____

<u>Isaiah 26:3</u>: You will keep him in perfect peace, whose mind is stayed on You, because he trusts in You.

<u>Hebrews 3:1 (NIV)</u>: Therefore, holy brothers, who share in the heavenly calling, fix your thoughts on Jesus, the apostle and high priest whom we confess.

Stay my mind on God; fix my thoughts on Jesus; then God will keep me in perfect peace. This is a clear picture: having peace will not happen by sitting back and waiting for God to just do it in me. I must choose it, I must do something about it. Stay, fix my mind; think on the right things—God, Jesus, and things above. I can't fill my mind with TV, all the bad on the evening news, and expect a peaceful night's sleep. I get it!

Your thoughts:

_____

_____

_____

_____

_____

_____

_____

_____

<u>Nehemiah 8:10b</u>: Do not sorrow, for the joy of the Lord is your strength.

I thank You, Lord, for Your mercy, grace, strength, and joy. Truly Your joy is my strength. You are my Savior, Lord, Master, Brother, Lover of my soul, Friend, and Strong Tower I can run into. All these things are causes of great joy—and I have joy in them. May You be exalted in my life, my family, my church, my community, and my nation!

Your thoughts:

_____

_____

_____

_____

_____

_____

_____

_____

<u>Luke 17:21 (KJV)</u>: ...behold, the kingdom of God is within you.

"Behold" is an instruction, something I'm being told to do. Since Jesus is the one saying this, it is all the more important. He wants me to understand that the kingdom is an internal rule. Knowing this should have significant bearing on my life and the choices I make: behavior, attitudes, and motives. Thank You, Lord, for Your word, which is true, to be believed, followed, and obeyed. We can trust it!

Your thoughts:

_____

_____

_____

_____

_____

_____

_____

Psalm 103:8 (ESV): The Lord is merciful and gracious, slow to anger and abounding in steadfast love.

Jonah 4:2b (ESV): ...for I knew that you are a gracious God and merciful, slow to anger and abounding in steadfast love.

O God, where would we be without Your mercy, grace and love? You know everything about us, and still You love us. Your ways are much higher than ours—they really are past finding out. I'm so grateful, Lord, that You are all we need. We can put our trust completely in You and You will never fail us. Thank You for Your steadfastness!

Your thoughts:

_____

_____

_____

_____

_____

_____

_____

_____

Romans 8:2: For the law of the Spirit of life in Christ Jesus has made me free from the law of sin and death.

Galatians 5:1 (NIV): It is for freedom that Christ set us free. Stand firm, then, and do not let yourselves be burdened again by a yoke of slavery.

Belonging to Jesus means I'm no longer under the law of sin and death. He has set me free for freedom. I'm now under the law of the Spirit of life and have the freedom to be and do everything Christ wants for me. Am I living a life of freedom? Does my life reflect this freedom to the people around me? I have freedom to serve Christ with my whole heart, am I? How can I partake more fully of the freedom for which Jesus made me free? Please give me Your wisdom, Lord!

Your thoughts:

_____

_____

_____

_____

_____

_____

_____

_____

<u>John 15:26 (NIV)</u>: "When the Counselor comes, whom I will send to you from the Father, the Spirit of truth who goes out from the Father, He will testify about Me."

Holy Spirit, thank You for being my Counselor and the Spirit of truth; thank You that You will testify about Jesus and that You will bring glory to Him by revealing Him to me. I also thank You that You'll keep my life in spiritual balance as I learn more to have a relationship with You. I know I'm going to be changed as I depend on You for that, be led as I surrender more fully to You, and be transformed by the renewing of my mind. Amen!

Your thoughts:

_____

_____

_____

_____

_____

_____

_____

_____

Psalm 148 is all about praise to God. Everything and everyone is to praise Him. The sun, moon, and stars because He created them and set them in place forever and ever. Sea creatures, elements, trees, animals, birds, kings, princes, rulers, young and old people because His name alone is exalted; His splendor is above Earth and heavens.

Lord, Your very Word not only commands praise to You, but it causes praise to You. I can't read about who You are and what You've done without praise just welling up and spilling out. You are an awesome God and worthy of all praise!

Your thoughts:

_____

_____

_____

_____

_____

_____

_____

_____

Job 19:25-27 (NIV): I know that my Redeemer lives, and that in the end He will stand upon the Earth. And after my skin has been destroyed, yet in my flesh I will see God; I myself will see Him with my own eyes. I, and not another. How my heart yearns within me!

It is an awesome thing, Lord, to know that even though we die, we live on with You eternally. What a marvelous plan You had, Father; a costly plan because it took the life of Your Son to make it come to pass. But He was raised again and so shall we be. We owe everything to You. Because of that, Lord, I surrender everything to You. Have Your way in me.

Your thoughts:

_____

_____

_____

_____

_____

_____

_____

_____

<u>Luke 4:1</u>: Then Jesus, being filled with the Holy Spirit, returned from the Jordan and was led by the Spirit into the wilderness...

Firstly, if Jesus needed to be filled with the Holy Spirit, how much more do I? Daily! Secondly, if being led by the Spirit, we may not expect to go into the wilderness. But we do, and we will, more than once. The promise was never that we wouldn't have troubles and problems, but that Jesus would be with us in them. We must learn to trust God and not self! He knows exactly what we need, and when, in order to mature us. I choose to trust You, Lord, because You are faithful!

Your thoughts:

_____

_____

_____

_____

_____

_____

_____

_____

<u>Psalm 43:5b (NIV)</u>: Put your hope in God, for I will yet praise Him, my Savior and my God.

I do put my hope in You, God. No matter what trial is going on, I can praise You because You are wise,

just,

loving,

merciful,

the Alpha and Omega,

the beginning and the end.

You know all things and You do all things well. How I love You, Lord!

Your thoughts:

_____

_____

_____

_____

_____

_____

_____

_____

1 Peter 2:9-10: But you are a chosen generation, a royal priest-hood, a holy nation, His own special people, that you may proclaim the praises of Him who called you out of darkness into His marvelous light; who once were not a people but are now the people of God, who had not obtained mercy but now have obtained mercy.

O God, I recognize and honor Your mercy given me in now belonging to You; and that You called me out of my darkness, depression, despair into the marvelous light of Christ my Savior, Priest, King. It's harder to grab onto being part of a royal priest-hood when I know my failures. I need to remember that I'm covered over with the blood of Jesus and it's His righteousness You see when You look at me. Thank You, God, that You have made us Your own special people. Hallelujah!

Your thoughts:

_____

_____

_____

_____

_____

_____

_____

_____

<u>Lamentations 2:19 (NIV)</u>: Arise, cry out in the night, as the watches of the night begin; pour out your heart like water in the presence of the Lord. Lift up your hands to Him for the lives of your children...

Not just our own children, Lord, but any child, any age, unsaved, new in the Lord, hungry, homeless, sick, naked, orphaned— there's no end to the needs. Give us Your heart for prayer, Lord; give us Your prayers, Holy Spirit, that we can know they will be answered. Take us out of ourselves and self-seeking, God, and put Your heart in us that we would truly love our neighbor as ourselves. This is Your plan!

Your thoughts:

_____

_____

_____

_____

_____

_____

_____

_____

<u>1 John 4:9-10</u>: In this the love of God was manifested toward us, that God has sent His only begotten Son into the world, that we might live through Him. In this is love, not that we loved God, but that He loved us and sent His Son to be the propitiation for our sins.

Hallelujah! What a Savior! God, thank You for Your great love that saved me and caused me to love You. Jesus, thank You that in You I live and move, and have my very being. Your plans are perfect, Lord. I pray to just fit in with them.

Your thoughts:

_____

_____

_____

_____

_____

_____

_____

_____

Micah 6:8 (NIV): He has showed you, O man, what is good. And what does the Lord require of you? To act justly and to love mercy and to walk humbly with your God.

O, Lord, if we just spent enough time with you, and walked humbly with You, knowing our need of Your salvation, Your grace, Your mercy, Your forgiveness, all else would fall into place. Holy Spirit, help us, help me, to do that. How we need You, Lord!

Your thoughts:

_____

_____

_____

_____

_____

_____

_____

_____

Colossians 2:6, 9-10: As you therefore have received Christ Jesus the Lord, so walk in Him... For in Him dwells all the fullness of the Godhead bodily; and you are complete in Him, who is the head of all principality and power.

O Jesus, truly You are all we need! We are safe in You; we can rely on You and trust in You because You are God. You are our victory over the evil one and we don't need to fear him. You are the author and finisher of our faith and so we are complete in You. Be my life, Jesus, that I truly may walk in You.

Your thoughts:

_____

_____

_____

_____

_____

_____

_____

_____

<u>Zephaniah 3:17 (NIV)</u>: The Lord your God is with you, He is mighty to save. He will take great delight in you, He will quiet you with His love, He will rejoice over you with singing.

O, God, Your promises make me weep. How can Almighty God, the Sovereign Lord, care this much about me? It is beyond my understanding; it is unsearchable. I can only choose to believe it because You put it in Your word and Your word is truth. Thank You, thank You, thank You for these precious promises!

Your thoughts:

_____

_____

_____

_____

_____

_____

_____

_____

Kay Smith Young

Jeremiah 9:23-24: Thus says the Lord: "Let not the wise man glory in his wisdom, let not the mighty man glory in his might, nor let the rich man glory in his riches; but let him who glories glory in this, that he understands and knows Me, that I am the Lord, exercising loving kindness, judgment, and righteousness in the Earth. For in these I delight," says the Lord.

It is the cry of my heart to know You, Lord. I have barely scratched the surface of knowing You. Some things about who You are:

You are love; Your ways are love.

You are peace; Your ways are peace.

You are a God of justice. Your ways are just.

You are my light and my salvation and the stronghold of my life.

There's no end to the learning about You. What an awesome God You are!

Your thoughts:

_____

_____

_____

_____

_____

_____

_____

Revelation 15:3-4: They sing the song of Moses, the servant of God, and the song of the Lamb, saying, "Great and marvelous are Your works, Lord God Almighty! Just and true are Your ways, O King of the saints! Who shall not fear You, O Lord, and glorify Your name? For You alone are holy. For all nations shall come and worship before You, for Your judgments have been manifested."

I know this is future, Lord, but what wonderful words—we can enjoy them now as well. Holy Lord, who was, is, and is to come, You are worthy to receive glory and honor and power. We bow our knees to You, King Jesus, and declare that You are Lord! We worship You through these words, God.

Your thoughts:

_____

_____

_____

_____

_____

_____

_____

_____

<u>Psalm 9:10</u>: And those who know Your name will put their trust in You; for You, Lord, have not forsaken those who seek You.

"Know" equals a relationship, walking with You, Lord, otherwise there is no trust. You are absolutely trustworthy so it's okay to put our trust in You. It is the only place where we never have to worry about what may happen with our trust. It can only be good because You are only good!

Your thoughts:

_____

_____

_____

_____

_____

_____

_____

<u>1 Thessalonians 4:16-18</u>: For the Lord Himself will descend from Heaven with a shout, with the voice of an archangel, and with the trumpet of God. And the dead in Christ will rise first. Then we who are alive and remain shall be caught up together with them in the clouds to meet the Lord in the air. And thus we shall always be with the Lord. Therefore comfort one another with these words.

We can comfort one another with these words, Lord, because they are spirit and they are life. What a blessing to know we will always be with You. I don't know how this will happen, or when, but I do know You, Lord, so I don't have to worry about it. Your promises are "Yes" and "Amen!" Thank You, Jesus, for taking away the fear of death for those who belong to You.

Your thoughts:

_____

_____

_____

_____

_____

_____

_____

<u>Psalm 103:1-3</u>: Bless the Lord, O my soul, and all that is within me, bless His holy name! Bless the Lord, O my soul, and forget not all His benefits: Who forgives all your iniquities, Who heals all your diseases.

O praise You, God. Your benefits are poured out on us. We're not even aware of some of them. Jesus provided the way so we could have relationship with You, and sent the Holy Spirit to lead us into all truth. He teaches us Your ways, God, and the more time we spend with You the more we know who You are. There is no end to Your benefits to us. Thank You seems so small for such big things, but we are eternally grateful!

Your thoughts:

_____

_____

_____

_____

_____

_____

_____

_____

<u>James 1: 2-4</u>: My brethren, count it all joy when you fall into various trials, knowing that the testing of your faith produces patience. But let patience have its perfect work, that you may be perfect [mature] and complete, lacking nothing.

When we first read the words "count it all joy when you fall into various trials," it doesn't compute, Lord. Even when we go on to verse three, "patience" doesn't seem like a great reward for trials. We have to keep going. We all probably would like the "mature and complete, lacking nothing" part. Along the way of the trial, if we're willing to move out of the self-pity and whining, we begin to see Your hand and realize You really do work all things for the good of those who love You and are called according to Your purpose (Romans 8:28).

Your thoughts:

_____

_____

_____

_____

_____

_____

_____

_____

Romans 1:16: For I am not ashamed of the gospel of Christ, for it is the power of God to salvation for everyone who believes, for the Jew first and also for the Greek.

Gospel: good news. Here's the key to salvation, Lord: believe! And of course we have to believe that Jesus died for our sin—it's personal. If we don't have Jesus, we don't have God either because He is the only way to God. It's not complicated, but sometimes people don't want it to be the only way. We have a choice to make, Lord, and since You don't change Your mind, I think we should choose Your way.

Your thoughts:

_____

_____

_____

_____

_____

_____

_____

_____

<u>Psalm 40:10</u>: I have not hidden Your righteousness within my heart; I have declared Your faithfulness and Your salvation; I have not concealed Your loving-kindness and Your truth from the great assembly.

This is the desire of my heart in writing this book, Lord. I pray that You will reveal Yourself to each person that reads it and that You will enable them to have their own "minute meditation" with You every day. Thank You for Holy Spirit's inspiration to me.

About the Author

Kay lives with her husband, Abe, in Poulsbo, Washington. They have been married 59 years, have four children, 15 grandchildren, and seven great-grandchildren. The love of her life, besides her Lord and her family, has been women's ministry and she has been active in several areas, especially Bible study. This is her first book.

CPSIA information can be obtained at www.ICGtesting.com
Printed in the USA
BVOW08s0217280114

343129BV00001B/2/P